A Taste of Crofting

Barbara Jane Gray asserts the moral right to
be identified as the author of this work
All rights reserved. No part of this publication may be
reproduced, stored in a retrieval system, or transmitted in any form or by
means, electronic, mechanical, photocopying, recording or otherwise,
without the prior permission of the publishers.

This first edition published November 2023

ISBN 978-1-7384141-3-0

Cover design – Tricky Imp
Other images – Various sources
Front cover image by the author.

More Information at: www.trickyimp.com

Printed in the United Kingdom by 4 Edge

A Taste of Crofting

A selection of recipes and information about crofting life.

Barbara Jane Gray

INDEX

Stews & Broths
Vegetable & Bere Stew 24
Onion Broth 25
Leek & Tattie Soup 27
Cock-A-Leekie Soup 29
Kale & Tattie Soup 31
Brussels Sprout Soup 33
Cream of Barley Soup 34
Cabbage Soup 35

Bannocks & Oatcakes
Early Unleavened Bannocks 43
Thin Bannocks 46
Bere Bannocks 47
Barbara's Vegan Bere Bannocks 48
Barbara's Best Beer Bere Bannocks 49
Quick & Easy Bannocks 50
Sautie Bannocks 51

Sour Dough Starter 53
Sour Dough Beremeal & Rye Bannocks 54
Beremeal Drop Scones 56
Beremeal Tattie Scones 57
Traditional Tattie Scones 58
Beremeal & Cheese Scones 59
Barbara's Beremeal & Sultana Scones 60
Girdle 'Drop' Scones 62

Beremeal Oatcakes	…………	63
Traditional Oatcakes	…………	64
Savoury Oatcakes	…………	65
Aberdeen Rowies	…………	66

Pies - Pastry

Shortcrust Pastry	…………	71
Wholemeal Shortcrust Pastry	…………	72
Beremeal Shortcrust Pastry	…………	73
Suet Pastry	…………	74
Cheesy Shortcrust Pastry	…………	75
Sweet Shortcrust Pastry.	…………	77

Pies – Pie Recipes

St Mary's Sausage meat, Apple & Onion Pie	..	78
Shepherd's Pie	…………	79
Forfar Bridies	…………	82

Fish

Crofter's Hotpot	…………	86
Crappit Heids	…………	87
Cullen Skink	…………	89
Smoked Haddock Kedgeree	…………	91
Herrings in Oatmeal	…………	92
Soused Herring	…………	93
Partan Bree	…………	94
Haggamuggie	…………	95

Meat
Haggis	…………	98
Inky Pinky	…………	100
Marag Dubh	…………	103

Cheese, Cream & Milk
Crowdie	…………	105
Fuarag	…………	106

Side Dishes & Other Savouries
Skirlie	…………	108
Clapshot	…………	109

Sweet Treats
Clootie Dumpling	…………	111
Broonie / Gingerbread	…………	112
Beremeal Gingerbread	…………	114
Beremeal Shortbread	…………	116
Traditional Shortbread	…………	117
Escape Cake	…………	118
Cranachan	…………	119
Scottish Tablet	…………	120
Butterscotch	…………	121

Beer & Other Drinks
Fisherman's Punch	…………	123
Deoch Bhan	…………	123
Athol Brose.	…………	124

Oats

Bere
(Artwork by Louise Bailey)

Oats along with Bere two of the most important crops
in the Highlands for centuries.

FOREWORD
by Peter Gray

There will always be room for debate about the diet of Crofters in the Highlands as each family would have their own unique take on how to cook, and what the ingredients would be. To a certain extent, the idea of set ingredients and method would not be something that the average crofter would subscribe to. Certainly, the diet of most crofting families would be bland and would include whatever they could lay their hands upon.

There is also a misconception about what the crofter would grow, this varied depending on the trends of the time. He gave his rent to the landowner, but generally he was also told what he could and couldn't grow. It wasn't the crofter's land and to a degree it wasn't the crofter's crop. This is because the crofter was just a tenant farmer with no business connections. As the sale of the crops was arranged by agents and factors to get the best prices within the best markets, the crofter would have no dealings in this. Of course, there were exceptions to this as confirmed by the frustrations of the Duke of Sutherland, commenting on certain crofters and their insistence on growing potatoes because there was less work involved. To a degree, this is why people starved during the potato famines. The over-reliance of certain crofters and landowners on potato growing caused overwhelming problems and only the crofts that included meal crops [mainly Oats and Bere] were able to produce anything at all. During the years of serious potato blight the crofters went hungry and even some of those who had managed to survive through the previous clearances were pushed to leave Scotland during this period.

Larger crofts may set aside some small plot for a few items for their own table but the small crofts had no such luxury and their entire, meagre plot of land was used for production of the crop the Laird required. This in no small part was due to the ridiculously small crofts allocated to the tenant. Between two and five acres of land were hopeless and even with larger plots, the crofter would struggle to produce enough to survive. This was by design, so that the landowner could ensure that the crofter and his family would have to work up to 200 days each year for the landowner. This forced slavery was a common practice and continued throughout the crofting period.

The crofter working by the coast may be tasked with working in the kelp trade but once the kelp industry collapsed, due to more modern methods of glass and soap making, these crofters were out of work. This had a large impact on many crofters and once again, they starved or moved on, many going overseas once more.

With this in mind, it is easy to see why the idea of recipes and methods of preparing and cooking food would be something that the crofting family would ignore. Oats, and obviously porridge was a staple and after all, no crofter needed to know how to make porridge or oat cakes.

Some crofters would keep three or four cattle, but at a time when there were no refrigerators, very little of what they produced could be kept and would have to be sold on. This was also true of the fisherman who would sell his catch but keep the offal which he would use for food, and sometimes it would be processed into oil. Many crofters lit their steadings with oil in 'cruise lamps' which burned this fish oil. Nothing was thrown away and everything was reused.

This publication is more to remind us how hard their life was and why there is little written or celebrated about this black period of Scotland's history. The recipes contained within are to let us understand the tastes and sometimes the methods with which, in times of plenty these ancestors of ours would make ends meet. And there were indeed times of plenty, often during major conflicts such as the French Revolutionary Wars of the late seventeen-hundreds, when Britannia needed everything she could get her hands on.

It is easy to see Crofting as somewhat romantic and many photographs can be found on the internet purporting to show the early crofters and their way of life. But we have to be reminded that all those photographs would be posed, and so you may not be seeing a true representation of their lifestyle and more of the wants and needs of the photographer. It was certainly not romantic. It was harsh, cruel and difficult to simply survive. The estimates of the numbers of Highlanders leaving to other countries is likely to be vastly incorrect as records could not be kept for such an exodus and there were likely far more than we think. What is known is that most of those who survived the trip to Canada, Australia or other far-away lands, found a better life than they previously had in the country of their birth.

In conclusion, the early crofter's diet was bland, but if we consider it compared with modern food, it was healthier and more nutritious. This is due to crops being grown on fertile soil not overworked or needing chemicals to enrich it. Neither was it over processed, containing all the chemicals and preservatives we seem to relish these days.

In conclusion. I think the title of the work says it all. It is a taste of those far off crofting days and not always a reproduction of the meals the crofter would eat.

Peter Gray – October 2023, Caithness, Scotland.

Lhaidhay Croft Museum

A Taste of Crofting

Introduction

Crofting is a way of farming rather than a period in time therefore, I have tried to focus on the more traditional, older recipes but have included a few more contemporary ones.

Whilst working as a curator of the Lhaidhay Croft Museum in Caithness, I researched a good deal about crofting life to help our visitors to have a more enjoyable visit. This included offering information about what they would eat and how they would cook their food, this depended upon the era and the type of person we were discussing, but with the Lhaidhay Croft, the fact that the food was always cooked over an open, peat fire with no advancement to a range or cooker, the method of this cooking was very similar to earlier practices and even the utensils and pans would be the same as hundreds of years previously.
It became very clear that our visitors would like a book with basic information about crofting life with more about the recipes that we would have seen from various times in history.

Crofting began early in Scottish history, around 1840 and continues today in the 21st century, with currently around 20,000 crofts in the Highlands and Islands still being registered, many of which do not make a good living from their land. It is good to see that the Crofting Commission are still supporting this traditional way of life to continue. The crofting Act was brought into force in 1886 to offer security to tenant farmers who had previously been persecuted during the Highland Clearances.

Did crofters share the same challenges as Townsfolk?

For most crofters, there would have been clean water, fresh air and at least some time during the winter months to recuperate. Although the short summer months of sowing, growing and harvesting times would have been busy, this was a very different lifestyle to townspeople who worked long hours throughout the year in unhealthy, dangerous and unsanitary surroundings. One bonus for crofters being that they could at least find peat for fuel and some wild foods for free in their locality, whereas people living in towns had to purchase everything they needed to survive, nothing came for free.

Considering the lack of population, there would be less likelihood for diseases to pass on as been the case in more cramped living conditions, such as would be experienced in busy towns and cities.

What would people eat?

From early times, crofters would have grown some crops, mainly oats and barley (or 'Bere' as it is known in the Highlands). There would likely be some cattle and sheep with a few chickens, but it would be very rare for crofters to eat beef, lamb or chicken as these were highly valued for trade. It is likely that most people would have a very plain diet, including oats, bere, some eggs, turnips, potatoes, kale, fish and onions plus anything they could forage from their land.

It is interesting to see that many crofters lived well into their 80s and 90s, I believe a lot of this was due to eating good diet, including oats, now considered a super food, barley (or Bere as it was known in Highlands) again, a very healthy grain with Bere being high in protein, low in gluten with a good fat content and many minerals important to healthy life.

I have included some of the basic recipes for broth, which were quite nutritious and surprisingly wholesome and filling.

Bread was rarely baked in ovens as most cooking would take place over an open fire and few people would have an oven until well into the 20th century, many not even having them into the 1960s! Bannocks would be cooked on a girdle or skillet over the fire and would not only be served with soups and broth but crumbled in to soups and porridge as a thickener.

Scones were popular, again being cooked on a girdle and having ingredients such as Beremeal, oats, eggs, cheese, onions, potatoes (or tatties) kale, wild fruits such as blaeberries, brambles, sloes, rowanberries (not very sweet but high in vitamin c) and occasionally sugar, I have tasted some of the earlier recipes for these scones and the Beremeal gives them an almost 'peaty' aroma and taste, very different to wheat scones. I think your opinion of Bare is akin to Marmite, you either love it or hate it, I LOVE IT!

What would the food be cooked in / on?

As mentioned earlier, the basic cooking equipment for any croft kitchen would include a girdle, a kettle and a cooking pot for broth and porridge. There would likely be a spurtle (or stick to stir the porridge), some form of tool to turn bannocks and scones (very much like our fish slice) with spoons and ladles made of metal or wood for stirring and serving.

(Artwork by Louise Bailey)

What did crofters drink?

As with most communities, brewing and distilling were very important parts of life, many long winter nights would be made far more pleasant by sampling a few drams or beers in front of the peat fires! We have included a few recipes for beers towards the rear of the book. Tea became important during the twentieth century and there might be some home pressed cider. Water would have been drunk if a local fresh water supply was available, usually a spring or well would be available, if not on the crofter's land, close-by as with Lhaidhay Croft.

I hope you enjoy reading this book and experimenting with the recipes! I have offered some traditional versions with more modern and some vegan ones as well, please try them and let me know what you think by visiting the publisher's website and send us a message at - www.trickyimp.com

Thank you.

Our Recipes Section

A Big Thank You

I have been very lucky to receive traditional recipes from people in Caithness and beyond, thanks to them all. You will find some very basic recipes which are traditional, others are more modern variations and even vegan options for you to try.

Thank you also to our brilliant artists! Sky and Isla Bain and Louise Bailey, they have helped to bring this book alive. Also, thanks to Freepik and other sources for their license free images.

Thanks to Peter Gray, author and historian for kindly writing the foreword.

The recipes sometimes ask for Beremeal, flakes or berries. These give a lovely earthy flavour to the food. We buy ours from a lovely traditional watermill on Orkney called Barony Mill who have an online shop, so it is worth looking them up on the internet to try this unique and healthy grain. You will see their advertisement and details at the rear of the book along with other suppliers of Beremeal and other ingredients you will need for the recipes. They have suppliers throughout the Highlands if you would like to browse their range.

Stews & Broth

(Artwork kindly provided by Louise Bailey)

Vegetable & Bere Stew

This is a tasty stew I have served up on several occasions, it makes a hearty meal served with bannocks, dumplings or on its own. In season, I always add chopped apples to the ingredients.

Ingredients
2 medium leeks (chopped)
2 medium Potatoes (peeled and cubed to your preferred size)
1 large Onion (Chopped to your preferred size)
2 medium Carrots (chopped to your preferred size)
Broth Mix -
> 2 Tbsp Bere Berries (I boil mine first for 5 minutes to prevent the stock in the stew from drying up)
> 2 Tbsp Dried peas, pearl barley. (I boil mine first for 5 – 10 minutes to prevent the stock in the stew from drying up).

2 ½ pints of Water
2 vegetable stock cubes
I add a good pinch of Sage to mine and a little gravy browning.
1 Tbsp. Oil to fry onions. Salt & pepper to taste.

Method

In a heavy bottomed large pan, fry the chopped onions until opaque. Add the leeks and continue to fry until tender. Add the potatoes and the stock cubes (dry) and fry gently until you see a film of starch forming on the potatoes, then add the sage if using and stir well.
I find the 'sweating' of the potatoes with the herbs and stock cube makes them more flavoursome.
Add the carrots and the boiled - dried broth mix with the water and top up with the additional water / stock. Simmer for around 1 ½ hours until the potatoes have slightly rounded edges.
Season with salt & pepper, then serve hot with a freshly baked bannock or dumplings.

<u>Onion Broth</u>

Ingredients
3 or 4 Medium to large Onions, chopped (half of them finely and the other half chunky)
2 Tbsp Oil
Gravy browning
2 Stock Cubes
1 Des sp sugar
Small glass of red wine (optional)
1 ½ pints hot water (potato water is good)
Handful of grated cheese to garnish.

Method

Use a heavy bottomed, large pan.

Chop half of the onions finely and fry in the hot oil until very dark brown, even slightly burned (gives more flavour).

Add the remaining larger pieces of onion and continue to fry on a lower heat until the larger onions become opaque.

Add the sugar and continue to caramelise the onions for 2 – 3 minutes.

As an option, I add a small glass of red wine to the onions which gives a really rich flavour.

In a separate jug, add the stock cubes to the hot water and stir until dissolved.

Add the stock to the onions.

Add a little of the gravy browning until you have a nice deep golden-brown colour.

Continue to simmer for an hour.

If possible, allow to stand an hour or overnight to allow the flavour to mature.

Reheat until piping hot and sprinkle a little grated cheese on top then serve with fresh bannocks or a handful of croutons.

Leek & Tattie Soup

Ingredients
2 large leeks washed and sliced approximately 1" lengths
2 large onions, chopped finely
2 medium potatoes, cubed into different size cubes.
2 pints milk (non-dairy oat milk works well)
1 pint water
1oz butter (vegan butter or margarine works well)
2 stock cubes
1 tsp Sage
salt & pepper to taste
I also use 2 to 3 heaped tablespoons of nutritional yeast to thicken and give a richer flavour.

Method
In a large pan melt the butter and gently fry the onions until opaque, add the leeks and continue to fry until soft.
Add the cubed potatoes (I use various sizes as some will then break down and thicken the soup naturally) Continue to stir and add the sage and stock cubes until the potatoes have a film of starch on them.
(if using the nutritional yeast, I add this at this stage too)

Add the water and milk and simmer for around an hour until the potatoes soften.
Add salt & pepper to taste.
I usually allow my soups to cool for at least a few hours before reheating and serving as this improves the flavour.
I serve with fresh bannocks or on its own as it is quite a hearty soup.

Cock – A – Leekie Soup

Another recipe that I could not miss out as I imagine over 90% of the UK population have heard of this hearty and traditionally Scottish soup.

Ingredients

4lb / 1.8kg oven ready chicken (or 500g Vegan Chicken Pieces)
1lb /500g Leeks Trimmed, washed and sliced into 1/2" / 12mm slices.
18 ready to eat Prunes.
1 large Onion peeled and chopped.
2 pints / 1 ltr Water
2 Tablespoons Long Grain Rice
2 Tablespoons chopped Fresh Parsley
a few stalks fresh Thyme
1 Bay Leaf
1 Stock Cube
Salt & Pepper to taste

Method

Place the chicken in the bottom of a large pan.

Cover with the water, add the Stock Cube and bring to the boil, removing any scum from the top.

Add the onion to the broth with the Bay Leaf and Thyme.

Add the leeks, prunes and rice and simmer gently for 15 – 20 minutes.

Lift the chicken out of the broth and serve either in pieces with the broth in the same dish or serve in a separate dish.

If using vegan chicken, begin the process by boiling the water, stock cube, onions, Bay Leaf and Thyme then adding the pieces and continue with the rest of the method.

Season to taste and serve hot with crusty bread.

Kale & Tattie Soup

Ingredients
Large bunch of kale, washed and shredded
2 large potatoes, cubed (with or without skins)
2 medium onions.
2 pints of good vegetable or leek/onion stock
handful of hedge garlic (or a clove of garlic)
oil to fry onions
salt & pepper to taste.

Method
Add the oil to a heavy bottomed pan and heat gently, add the diced onions and garlic clove if using, fry for a few minutes until soft.
Add the potatoes to the onions and stir for a few minutes on a low heat.
Add the kale stirring for a minute or so.
If using Hedge Garlic, add it at this stage.
Add the stock and simmer for around 45 minutes to an hour or until the potatoes are soft.
You can thicken with a little flour and water paste / gravy granules or let the potatoes soften and disperse into soup to make it naturally thicker.
Add salt & pepper to taste and serve piping hot.

The next few soup and broth recipes were copied from a book in the Lhaidhay Museum, dated 1911 called 'The Woman's Book, contains everything a woman ought to know'.
This book was a very popular artefact in the museum and was commented upon by many of our visitors, both male and female. Published by T C & E C Jack, 67 Long Acre W.C and Edinburgh.
It was edited by Florence B Jack, late principal of the Domestic Arts, Edinburgh and Rita Strauss, assisted by many expert contributors.'

(Notes in italics and brackets are from the editor with options or conversions in measures).

Of all the artefacts in the museum, I think this has to be one of the most popular. Many husbands and partners have commented (to their later cost no doubt) that their wife / partner could do with a copy!! Maybe if we could have a reprint made there would be quite an interest to buy it.

Brussel Sprout Soup

Ingredients
1lb Brussel Sprouts
1 gill *(¼ pint)* of Cream or ½ pint Boiled Milk
1 quart *(2 pints)* White Stock
Pepper & Salt to taste

Method
Trim the Brussels Sprouts, cutting away and decayed or discoloured leaves, wash well and let steep in a basin of cold water with a few drops of vinegar for half an hour.
Then drain and throw into a saucepan of fast boiling water (salted in a proportion of one (level) dessert spoon to one quart (2 pints)
Adding also, a small piece of washing soda ***Please note this is not wash powder!!*** (bicarbonate of soda – a pinch)

Boil quickly with the lid off from fifteen to twenty minutes, removing any scum that may rise. Do not overcook the sprouts, or their colour will be destroyed. When ready, drain and rub through a fine wire sieve. Put the stock into the saucepan, add the Brussel sprout puree, cream or milk and seasoning and make quite hot, but do not boil again.

Cream of Barley Soup

Ingredients
1 quart of chicken or veal Boilings *(A vegetable stock will be a good substitute)*
2 oz Pearl Barley *(or Bere Berries if you have them)*
1 gill *(½ pint)* of cream or ½ pint boiled milk *(non-dairy milk or cream may be used)*
1oz Butter
1 Onion
½ " Cinnamon stick
1 Bay Leaf
A few Parsley stalks.

Method
Use the fine Barley for this soup
Wash it well in cold water. Put into a saucepan with cold water to cover, bring to the boil, strain and rinse again with cold water This is to blanch or whiten the barley.
Rinse out the saucepan and return the barley to it with the meat boilings or thin white stock.
(The water in which a fowl, rabbit or piece of veal has been boiled can be used for this soup) (*a good vegetable stock will also be quite acceptable).*
Add the onion, thinly sliced, the Bay leaf, cinnamon and parsley stalks. Simmer for 2 hours or until the barley is quite cooked.

Then rub as much as possible through a Tammy cloth or hair sieve. *(Flour sieve)*

Return the puree to the pan with the butter, and add the cream, or boiled milk. Season to taste, and stir over the fire until boiling.

A few cooked green peas or asparagus points may be added.

Cabbage Soup

Ingredients
1 Cabbage
1 Small onion or leek
1 quart (2 pints) meat boilings
½ pint milk
1 Tablespoon crushed Tapioca
1 tea-spoonful of chopped Parsley
Some croutons of toasted bread
(editor's note – Toasted Oatcake does well as a replacement).

Method
Wash the cabbage well in cold water, and remove the coarse outside leaves and any hard pieces of stalk. Separate all the leaves, and let them soak in cold water and salt for half an hour. Then drain the water away, and shred the leaves finely.

Put the shred cabbage into a saucepan of fast boiling water, salted in the proportion of one dessert spoonful to the quart, boil quickly for five minutes, and then drain. Slice the onion or leek very thinly, and chop it finely, put it into the saucepan with the cabbage and stock or meat boilings, and simmer for twenty minutes. Add the milk and crushed tapioca, and cook for ten minutes longer or until the tapioca turns quite clear. Add the parsley just before serving, and season to taste with white pepper and salt. Put some small croutons of toasted bread into the soup-tureen, and pour the soup, boiling hot over them.

I think that some of these recipes might be a little grand for most Crofting wives but the main part of the ingredients would likely be used to make tasty and inexpensive soup).

(Artwork kindly provided by Skye Bain)

Scottish Oats

Oats have been grown and have been a staple of the Highlands for hundreds of years and though the variety of oats have changed, they remain basically the same crop. Black Oats, sometimes called Japanese Oats, were the original crop grown by crofters in most areas, and over the years the methods of growing this crop has changed little. Its importance to the livelihood of the crofter and economy of the area cannot be overstated, 'meal' as it was generally known, was exported south by ship and eventually by rail through the period.

Black Oats are now grown mainly as a soil improver but the type is hardy and prolific with the possibility of becoming a weed in other crops if not managed well.

Today, there is still a large demand for oats and Scottish porridge has become well known all over the world.

Though the Scottish oatcake is still made and eaten all around the country, other areas of Britain have become fond of oats due to the unique flavour and nutritional value, and the Midlands of England developed their own soft oatcake which is one of the tastiest ways of eating this versatile crop.

Oats can be grown on ground that is unsuitable for other crops and can withstand a variety of unpleasant environments yet still give a reasonable yield, this made it ideal for the Scottish climate. Now known as a 'superfood', oats are not to be underestimated in their value to our diet and were partly responsible in lessening the effect of the two great potato famines in Scotland. In Ireland, the blight of the potato caused a great deal of problems to the poorer people and many starved as the potato crop rotted, yet in Scotland the dependency in the potato hadn't been so great due to the 'meal' trade and so the famine wasn't quite as severe in some areas.

As to be expected, many recipes have been developed from the use of oats but the most common uses in the crofting community were in two particular dishes, the first was the Scottish Oatcake, the second, Porridge. It may be a little extravagant to call them 'dishes', as these two items were a daily staple, they provided a nutritious, easy meal out to the fields with them.

THE OATCAKE

The Scottish oatcake was easy and simple to produce but that isn't to say that each family didn't have their own additions to make it more interesting. The basic ingredient was oats, mixed with water, butter or lard and salt it was kneaded and rolled into a large flat pancake. This was then dropped onto a 'girdle' or frying pan and cooked until hard on both sides. There was also a purpose-built girdle for toasting oatcakes, similar to the rare item at Lhaidhay Croft Museum in Caithness.

(Artwork kindly provided by Louise Bailey)

The Lhaidhay toasting Girdle

The oatcakes would sometimes be scored into what are called 'farles' so that good size pieces could be broken and then stored ready for use.

PORRIDGE

Porridge used more or less the same ingredients as the oatcakes but was made similar to a gruel. Again, everyone had their own way of making it and sometimes whey or milk was added but the basic ingredients were oats in water seasoned with salt.

These days, porridge tends to be eaten as a sweet dish but through most of the crofting communities it was considered a more savoury meal and could on occasions include onions and other scraps of vegetables.

Of worthwhile note, is the mention of the Porridge Drawer which may bring memories back to those readers of a certain age.

The Porridge Drawer was indeed a drawer in a dresser or similar in which, after a good clean out, a cauldron full of porridge was poured whilst still warm. The porridge was allowed to set and then later could be cut, or parts broken off to be eaten on its own or with other food. The crofter would find it a convenient way to take food easily out into the fields without the need to cook. Children would also be able to get food whenever they found the need. If the crofter had the old type of 'box bed' in the house with a drawer underneath, a novel tradition was to pour the porridge before going to bed which would provide under-bed heating.

This particular drawer could also be used for the new bairn (baby) to be placed in as it made an excellent crib by the side of the bed, and indeed I have spoken with quiet a few people who remember this practice.

Bannocks & Oatcakes

(Artwork kindly provided by Louise Bailey)

'One – Pot' cooking as we now call it, was a necessity when the only form of heat, therefore, only 'cooker' was an open peat fire. This didn't deter the 'wifey' from having a variety of food available throughout the year. One of the staples in any crofting diet was the Bannock, soda type bread which was cooked on a girdle or skillet. The bannock could be anything from a thin, Chapati style flat bread to a thicker, more robust 'cake' used with broths and stew to make the meal more filling and, when drier, it was also crumbled into porridge.

The original Bannock would have been unleavened, this was very filling and quite a heavy form of bread. Later, the introduction of bicarbonate of soda, made the bread lighter.

Oatcakes were an essential part of the crofter's diet, they last well and were easy to wrap up and take out to the fields. Like the Bannocks, they were often crumbled into porridge to make a more satisfying meal.

Scottish Scones were made on the girdle or skillet and unlike English scones, were made with a batter of 'dropping' consistency and were either savoury, plain or sweet. I have added some recipes for baked scones though as they are too good to miss out.

Early - Unleavened Bannocks

Ingredients
300ml Buttermilk (or any plant milk)
1 oz (25g) Butter
4oz (115g) Beremeal
¼ tsp Salt *(Likely more than this in the traditional recipe as salt was much loved by Highland Crofters if they had some spare!)*

Method
Put the milk into a pan with the butter. Add the salt and heat until the butter has melted but make sure the mixture doesn't boil.
Add the beremeal until it makes a soft dough.
Turn the dough onto a board with a covering of beremeal and gently knead it into a ball. Roll out making a round shape, approximately 11" or 28cm diameter.
Heat a girdle or skillet, but make sure it is not too hot by testing with a small amount of beremeal, if it burns, it is too hot!
Place the bannock on the girdle / skillet (it can be moved by supporting it over a rolling pin).
Cook for approximately 5 minutes then lift with a fish slice and turn over.
When both sides are brown, tap the bottom with your knuckle and if cooked, it will sound hollow.

Eat with butter or plain but use within 24 hours for the best results.

Thin Bannocks

This recipe was kindly provided by Anne McLennan

Ingredients
4oz Beremeal
3 Eggs
1 oz Butter (melted)
Pinch Salt
Water to mix

Method
In a bowl, mix the beremeal and salt.
Whisk the eggs until fluffy and add with the melted butter, to the beremeal.
Add enough water to the paste to make a thin pouring batter (As for pancakes).
Using a ladle or pour from a jug on to a hot girdle or skillet. If the batter does not spread, it can be eased with a pallet knife or fish slice. The heat will stop the mixture from spreading too far.
Flip the pancake over once it has browned. The mixture will rise a little on the skillet / girdle.
Once cooked on both sides, place on a warm tray and serve with butter or for a special treat, butter and jam / marmalade.

Bere Bannocks

Ingredients
Self Raising flour
1/2lb beremeal
1 teaspoon baking soda
½ teaspoon salt
Buttermilk (or any plant milk)

Method
Mix all dry ingredients in a bowl. Add enough buttermilk to make a soft dough, knead a little but not too much as the bannock could become rubbery.
Shape the bannocks on a board dusted with beremeal.
Bake on a medium hot girdle until light brown, tur. over and cook the other side.
When cooked, the bannock should sound hollow when tapped.
Serve warm or cold but preferably the same day as cooked.

Barbara's Vegan Bere Bannocks

Ingredients
6oz Bread Flour
4oz Beremeal
1oz Vegan Butter
6 fl oz Oat milk
1tsp Bicarbonate of Soda
½ tsp Cream of Tartar.
Pinch Salt

Method
In a pan, heat the Oat milk and butter until warm, add the bicarbonate of soda and cream of tartar, (this will fizz so a large pan is ideal).
In a large bowl (I use an old fashioned, brown and cream pancheon) place the meal and flour with the liquid ingredients to make a soft dough. Mix together and turn out onto a board dusted with beremeal.
Knead lightly to form your bannocks, either two large or four smaller ones.

Place the bannocks on a heated skillet or girdle, cook until brown (around 5 – 7 minutes) and turn over. Once cooked, the bannock should sound hollow when tapped with your knuckles.
Serve warm with vegan butter, cheese or with your chosen stew.

Barbara's Best Beer Bere Bannocks (Quite a tongue twister!)

Anyone who knows me, is aware that I enjoy a glass of beer when I'm baking, this is a great excuse for me to have a sample before it goes into the recipe!

Ingredients
4oz Strong White Bread Flour
2oz Beremeal
3 fluid oz Beer (I use a darker beer but any will do)
½ tsp Bicarbonate of soda
Pinch Cream of Tartar
Pinch Salt

Method
Mix all the dry ingredients together.
Add the beer (Best freshly opened) and mix the ingredients into a soft dough (May take a little more or less beer).
Knead gently on a surface with a sprinkle of beremeal, into a smooth ball. Cut into two pieces and form into rounds. Using a rolling pin, roll out to approximately 1" (25mm) thick.
 Lay the bannocks on a heated skillet or girdle, cook until brown (around 5 – 7 minutes) and turn over. Once cooked, the bannock should sound hollow when tapped with your knuckles.

Serve warm with vegan butter, cheese or with your chosen stew and with the remainder of the beer of course!

Quick and Easy Bannock

Ingredients
2oz Self Raising flour
2oz Beremeal
Pinch Bicarbonate of Soda
Pinch Salt
Warm Milk to mix

Method
Mix all the ingredients in a bowl and knead lightly until you make a smooth dough. It should be slightly sticky to ensure the bannock is not too dry when cooked.
Make into a round and roll out until approximately 1" or 25mm thick.
Turn out on to a hot skillet or girdle and cook until brown on both sides.
Easy recipe that is quick and easy to make every day. Serve fresh and warm.

Sautie Bannocks

Sautie is from the Gaelic, for Soot "suidh".
These bannocks were traditionally made for Bannock Nicht, or Shrove Tuesday. Made by an unmarried girl and traditionally the maker was not allowed to speak whilst making the bannocks, the other girls would tease her to try and make her talk. A ring would be placed in the batter and the lucky single girl to find it would then be next married.
A similar bannock was served for Halloween (Samhain Bannock) and this would have some soot in the ingredients. The single girls would each take a piece to bed with them at night and place it under their pillow, hopefully to dream about their future husband.

Ingredients
2oz Oatmeal (fine)
2oz Plain flour
1 tablespoon Treacle or syrup
½ tsp bicarbonate of soda
1 tsp cream of Tartar
1 egg. (Vegan egg replacer works well)
Sour milk
Pinch salt

Method
Mix dry ingredients in a bowl. Add the treacle, egg and milk to form a smooth batter of single cream consistency.
Pour into a jug.
Heat a girdle or skillet until quite hot but not smoking. Using a tablespoon, drop the batter over the convex side to form a nice round shape.
Once cooked, flip over and cook the opposite side.
Cool on a wire tray and serve fresh.

Sour Dough Starter with Rye flour (or any good quality bread flour)

A sour dough starter can take 10 days to create but is well worth the time and it can be kept for many weeks and 'brought bake to life' so to speak by 'feeding' with more flour and water.
I have only recently started making sour dough bread and find the method is not only traditional but the bread has more flavour than conventional baker's yeast bread.

To make a sour dough 'starter' -

Day 1
In a sterilised glass jar or a bowl with a well-fitting lid (do not use aluminium bowls or containers)
Mix well - 3 ½ oz / 100g Rye flour with 3 ½ fl oz / 100ml of water.
Leave for 3 days at room temperature

Day 3
Mix in 1 ¾ oz / 50g of Rye flour and 1 ¾ fl oz / 50ml of water.
Cover and leave for 2 days

Repeat this for Day 5 and Day 7

Cont …

Day 10
The starter should now smell pleasant, not vinegary or harsh. The starter can actually last for years if you continue feeding it every two to three days and keep at room temperature with a lid on.
The starter can be kept 'dormant' in the fridge for up to four weeks and fed weekly. It can even be frozen and brought back to life by feeding and bringing back to room temperature.

Sour Dough Beremeal and Rye Bread

Ingredients
Day 1
2 oz / 60g Starter
11 oz / 320g Beremeal
14fl oz/ 400ml Cold Water

Method
Mix together thoroughly either by hand or using a stand mixer and dough hook.
Cover and leave overnight at room temperature.

Day 2
Add an additional
11oz / 320g Beremeal
11oz / 320g Rye Flour
14fl oz / 400ml warm water (blood heat)
2 tsp / 10g Salt

Mix all the ingredients together in a large mixing bowl or using a dough hook in a stand mixer.
Combine until you have a soft, smooth dough,
Place all the dough on a floured worktop and knead for around 25 minutes until the dough is pliable and smooth (if using the stand mixer, use a slow speed for around 15 - 20 minutes).

Divide the dough in two and shape ready for baking, they can be baked as rounds on a flat tin, or as loaves in 2lb loaf tins.
Place in a pre-heated oven 210 / 450 / gas 8 and bake for 25 minutes, cover the loaf with foil or greaseproof paper and continue to bake for a further 25 to 30 minutes.
When baked, the underside of the loaf should sound hollow when you tap it with your knuckles. Remove from tins and cool on a rack.
This is gorgeous freshly baked and will freeze well.

Beremeal Drop Scones
This recipe was kindly provided by Margaret Walker

Ingredients
4oz (115g) Beremeal
1/2oz (15g) Sugar
½ tsp Bicarbonate of soda
1 egg
pinch salt
Milk to mix
Butter to cook

Method
Sift the dry ingredients into a bowl.
Add the egg and slowly mix in the milk to make a batter, consistency similar to double cream. Heat the girdle or skillet and brush with a little of the butter. Drop a tablespoonful of the batter to the hot skillet / girdle. Cook until brown them flip over to cook evenly on both sides.
Serve hot with butter, with Jam or marmalade for a treat.

Beremeal Tattie Scones

Ingredients
6 oz (175g) floury mashed potatoes
2oz (60g) Beremeal
1 oz (25g) Butter
Pinch Salt

Method
Mix all ingredients together to form a dough.
Lightly coat a board or worktop with beremeal and place the dough upon it and gently knead it. Divide the mixture in two.
Roll half of the dough out forming a circular shape to around 1/4" (5mm) thick
Score the circle into 1/4s

Place on a medium hot skillet or girdle and cook until brown, toss over with a fish slice or pallet knife and cook until golden brown.
Serve hot with butter.

(Artwork kindly provided by Iona Bain)

Traditional Tattie Scones

Ingredients
1lb (500g) Floury Potatoes
4oz (125g) Plain Flour
1oz Butter (optional)
Pinch Salt.

Method
Peel the potatoes and cut into squares (approximately 1 ½ " or 45mm square) Boil the potatoes until tender. Mash until smooth and add the butter with the salt. Allow to cool.
Add the flour and mix into a paste, this should not be sticky so sometimes a little more flour may be required.

Put the mixture onto a floured board and roll out to approximately 1/2" or 1cm. Score into quarters (not right through the scone, this is just to mark it.
Place on a hot girdle or skillet and cook each side until golden brown.
These are great to serve immediately or will freeze well. When I reheat mine, I either warm in a toaster for a few minutes or in a skillet with butter to make them golden and luxurious.
Can be eaten with extra butter or with a breakfast to make a really hearty meal.

Beremeal and Cheese Scones

Ingredients
12oz SR Flour
12oz Beremeal
8 oz strong cheese
300ml Milk
1oz Butter (melted)
2 Eggs
2 tsp Baking Powder
1 tsp salt
¼ tsp white pepper
(Optional - add 1oz finely chopped Onion or Leeks the eggs can be replaced with 1 tsp baking powder and a dash of vinegar in the milk)

Method
Sift all the dry ingredients in to a bowl and mix well. Rub in the butter.
Add the wet ingredients, to form into soft dough. Do not over handle the dough but shape into a round and roll out to approximately 1 ½ " thick.
Using a cutter or a glass, cut the dough into circles. Place on a lightly greased baking tray and cook in a preheated oven 350 degrees F / 180 degrees C / 170 degrees C for Fan oven / gas mark 4 – 5
Bake for around 12 -15 minutes until golden brown and slightly firm to the touch.

Break or cut in half and serve warm or cold with butter.

Barbara's Beremeal and Sultana Scones
This recipe was mentioned to me by a visitor to Lhaidhay Croft Museum. He said that once he had sampled Beremeal Scones, he would never go back to plain Wheat Scones. Once I tasted them, I understood why. They are a little heavier than traditional wheat scones but the flavour is superb!

Ingredients
8oz SR Flour
2 oz Beremeal
2 oz Caster Sugar
2oz Butter.

2oz Sultanas
1/2 tsp Baking Powder
Pinch Salt
Milk (Alternatively use Plant milk or Lemonade / tonic Water to mix -
I use lemonade as it acts well as a raising agent and makes the scones a little lighter and sweeter than milk).

Method
Sift the flour, beremeal, baking powder and salt into a bowl. Rub the butter into the dry ingredients until it forms a breadcrumb like consistency. Add the sugar and sultanas and mix well.
Add the liquid until you have a light but not sticky, soft dough. Do not over handle as this will prevent the dough from rising well. If you have time, the dough should be covered with cling wrap and put in the refrigerator for 1-2 hours.
Gently roll out to approximately 2" thick and cut into circles with a pastry cutter or glass. Should make 10 – 12 scones depending on the size of your cutter.
Place on a lightly greased baking tray and bake in a preheated oven 425 F / 200 degrees C / Gas7 for 15 – 20 minutes until brown.

I love these with fresh butter and Scottish Raspberry jam!

Girdle 'Drop' Scones

Ingredients
8ox Plain flour
1 egg (beaten) Vegan egg replacer does the job too
1 oz butter / margarine
1 teaspoon cream of tartar
½ tsp bicarbonate of soda
pinch salt
Milk to mix

Method
Sieve all dry ingredients into a bowl
Rub in the butter / margarine.
Mix in the milk and egg until you have a batter the consistency of double cream. Pour the batter in to a jug for pouring.
Heat your girdle / skillet until hot and pour a small amount of your batter onto it, the batter will spread to make rounds. Once browned, flip over with a pallet knife or fish slice and cook until brown.
It is best to make several at a time, usually approximately 3" - 31/2" diameter and once cooked, stack and keep warm until served.
Serve warm with butter and jam.

Beremeal Oatcakes

Ingredients
4 oz Oatmeal
3oz Beremeal
Pinch Salt
1/4 tsp bicarbonate of soda
2 tablespoons Butter (melted) or oil
Water to mix

Method
Mix all the dry ingredients in a bowl, add the melted butter/oil and water until you have a pliable dough and turn out on to a beremeal covered surface. Knead the dough gently until it is handleable and not separating. Roll out the dough until it is approximately 1/8" or 3mm thick.
With a pastry cutter or glass, cut into rounds approximately 3" diameter.
Place on a hot girdle or skillet and cook until it starts to brown, carefully flip over and continue to cook until the 'cakes' are firm to touch. Cool on a wire rack.
Serve with butter and cheese. These can be stored and toasted to enhance the flavour.

Traditional Oatcakes

Ingredients
5 oz / 140 g Rolled Oats
5 oz / 140g Oatmeal
3 oz / 75g Butter
¾ tsp Salt
100 – 150ml Boiling water

Method
Mix all the dry ingredients together, melt the butter into100ml of the boiling water to start, add the remainder of the water to make a firm dough (add more water if needed).
Turn out onto a surface sprinkled with oatmeal and knead the dough until it is an even texture.
Roll out the dough until it is approximately 1/8" / 3mm thick.
With a pastry cutter or glass, cut into rounds approximately 3" / 7.5cm diameter.
Place on a hot girdle or skillet and cook until it starts to brown, carefully flip over and continue to cook until the 'cakes' are firm to touch. Cool on a wire rack.
Serve with butter and cheese. These can be stored and toasted to enhance the flavour.

Savoury Oatcakes

Ingredients
5 oz / 140 g Rolled Oats
5oz / 140g Oatmeal
3oz / 75g Butter or 75ml Oil
1 Tablespoon Dried Leeks or Onion Granules
1 heaped teaspoon Sage
¾ tsp Salt
100 – 150ml Boiling water

Method
Mix all the dry ingredients together, melt the butter into100ml of the boiling water to start, add the remainder of the water to make a firm dough (add more water if needed).
Turn out onto a surface sprinkled with oatmeal and knead the dough until it is an even texture.
Roll out the dough until it is approximately 1/8" or 3mm thick.
With a pastry cutter or glass, cut into rounds approximately 2" / 5cm diameter.
Place on a hot girdle or skillet and cook until it starts to brown, carefully flip over and continue to cook until the 'cakes' are firm to touch. Cool on a wire rack.
Serve with butter and cheese. These can be stored and toasted to enhance the flavour.

Aberdeen Rowies

Read all the instructions before making this recipe to ensure you understand it well.

Ingredients
1lb / 450g of plain flour
2 tsp of sea salt
6oz / 160g of lard or white vegetable shortening
6oz /160g of butter
240ml of lukewarm water
1oz / 25g of fresh yeast or 7g of fresh yeast
1 tbsp of caster sugar

Method
In a jug with capacity for at least 500ml liquid as the 'froth' may take up this space. Mix the yeast and half of the sugar with the warm water and leave in a warm place until frothy. It must not be hot, hand warm is perfect.
Add the salt, flour and the remaining sugar to a large mixing bowl and mix through.
Add in the yeast and water to the flour and blend through to create a dough. It might be a little sticky but that is fine.
Place in a clean oiled bowl and leave to rise in a warm place for 1 hour.

After the hour, blend the lard / shortening and butter together to form one mass in a separate bowl. I find doing this by hand is best. Split the blended fat into three 'chunks' and set aside in the bowl.

Split the dough in three and roll out one third flat across a well-floured wooden board or surface into a rough rectangular shape about 1/2inch thick.

Using your hands, smear one third of the butter and lard 'chunk' over the lower two thirds of your rectangle. Fold the top half (without the mixture) over onto the middle third, and then the bottom third up on top of that.

Wait approximately half an hour and repeat the process again, but roll the dough the opposite way to how you have folded it. Wait another half hour and repeat for the last time, turning the dough again to roll the opposite way.

You are basically creating layers in the pastry with the butter/lard mixture in between.

Split the dough into balls and stretch to form rough circular shapes. They are not perfectly round so a rough circle is perfect. They also should not be perfectly flat on the top either and have some kind of texture.

Repeat with the other two pieces of dough and place all the circular Rowies on a greased baking sheet or paper.

Leave to rise for a further 30 minutes and preheat the oven to 180c (fan). Bake in a hot oven 180c (fan) for 15 minutes & then 160c for 10minutes.
Eat immediately out of the oven or leave to cool completely for storing.

Savoury Pies

Where would we be on a cold, wintry day without a wholesome and filling pie? Although some of these recipes are not necessarily 'Crofting' based, they cannot be missed out of my book as they are so archetypally Scottish and would be eaten many years ago and indeed still are, in the more modern twentieth century Croft.

All good pies need great pastry!

Author's note -
I use Self Raising flour for most of my pastry, if you don't have any, then you can use plain flour with 1 level teaspoon of Baking Powder to each 3 ½ oz / 100g flour sifted and mixed well.

Here are some traditional shortcrust pastry recipes, some with a little twist that you might not have come across before.

I use my stand mixer or food processor for most of my 'rubbing in' for pastry, biscuits and cake. It makes a good job and is less taxing on my bad back!

Shortcrust Pastry

Ingredients.
1lb / 500g White Self Raising Flour
8 oz / 250g Cold Vegan or other Butter
3 1/2 fl oz / 100ml Really Cold Water (approximately)
Pinch salt and white pepper

Method
Make sure your hands and all utensils are nice and cold before you start.
Sift the flour, salt and pepper into a mixing bowl.
Cut the butter into cubes and rub into the dry ingredients to form a breadcrumb-like consistency.
With a cold flat bladed knife, mix the ingredients whilst pouring in half of the water and, little by little, mix the ingredients into a soft dough.
The dough should not be sticky but should leave the bowl clean around the edges when mixed.
Cover with cellophane and let stand, preferably in a fridge for an hour.
Lightly cover your work surface with flour and place the dough on the flour.
With a floured rolling pin, roll out the pastry to approximately ¼" or 6 mm thick to your desired shape / size.
For a more solid pastry, plain flour can be used.
Bake as per the recipe instructions, usually 180 / 350 / gas 4 for around 30 minutes

Wholemeal Shortcrust Pastry

Ingredients.
1lb / 500g Wholemeal Self Raising Flour
8 oz / 250g Cold Vegan or other Butter
3 1/2 fl oz / 100ml Really Cold Water (approximately)
Pinch salt and white pepper

Method
Make sure your hands and all utensils are nice and cold before you start.
Sift the flour, salt and pepper into a mixing bowl.
Cut the butter into cubes and rub into the dry ingredients to form a breadcrumb-like consistency.
With a cold flat bladed knife, mix the ingredients whilst pouring in half of the water and, little by little, mix the ingredients into a soft dough.
The dough should not be sticky but should leave the bowl clean around the edges when mixed.
Cover with cellophane and let stand, preferably in a fridge for an hour.
Lightly cover your work surface with flour and place the dough on the flour.
With a floured rolling pin, roll out the pastry to approximately ¼" or 6 mm thick to your desired shape / size.
For a more solid pastry, plain flour can be used.
Bake as per the recipe instructions, usually 180 / 350 / gas4 for around 30 minutes

Beremeal Shortcrust Pastry

One of my favourite pastries for a vegan version of Mince and Onion Pie!

Ingredients.
12 oz / 340g White Self Raising Flour
4oz / 125g Beremeal
8 oz / 250g Cold Vegan or other Butter
3 1/2 fl oz / 100ml Really Cold Water (approximately)
Pinch salt and white pepper

Method

Make sure your hands and all utensils are nice and cold before you start.
Sift the flour, salt, pepper and beremeal into a mixing bowl.
Cut the butter into cubes and rub into the dry ingredients to form a breadcrumb-like consistency.
With a cold flat bladed knife, mix the ingredients whilst pouring in half of the water and, little by little, mix the ingredients into a soft dough.
The dough should not be sticky but should leave the bowl clean around the edges when mixed.
Cover with cellophane and let stand, preferably in a fridge for an hour.
Lightly cover your work surface with flour and place the dough on the flour.

With a floured rolling pin, roll out the pastry to approximately ¼" or 6 mm thick to your desired shape / size.

Using Self Raising flour makes the flour lighter as it actually rises during baking.

For a more solid pastry, plain flour can be used.

Bake as per the recipe instructions, usually 180 / 350 / gas4 for around 30 minutes

Suet Pastry

This is a very hearty and surprisingly light pastry, great for topping such as mince and onion and meat & potato fillings.

Ingredients
8oz SR Flour
8oz Vegetarian Suet (lighter than the beef version but this can be used)
3 1/2 fl oz / 100ml Really Cold Water (approximately)
Pinch of salt & white pepper

Method
Sift the flour, salt & pepper into a mixing bowl.
Mix in the suet into the flour thoroughly
With a cold flat bladed knife, mix the ingredients whilst pouring in half of the water and, little by little, mix the ingredients into a soft dough.

The dough should not be sticky but should leave the bowl clean around the edges when mixed.

Cover with cellophane and let stand, preferably in a fridge for an hour.

Lightly cover your work surface with flour and place the dough on the flour.

With a floured rolling pin, roll out the pastry to approximately 1/2" or 12 mm thick to your desired shape / size.

Using Self Raising flour makes the flour lighter as it actually rises during baking.

Bake as per the recipe instructions, usually 180 / 350 / gas4 for around 30 minutes.

Cheesy Shortcrust Pastry

Ingredients.

1lb / 500g White Self Raising Flour
8 oz / 250g Cold Vegan or other Butter
4oz / 125g Grated strong Cheese (vegan or dairy)
3 1/2 fl oz / 100ml Really Cold Water (approximately)
Pinch salt and white pepper

Method

Make sure your hands and all utensils are nice and cold before you start.
Sift the flour, salt and pepper into a mixing bowl.
Cut the butter into cubes and rub into the dry ingredients to form a breadcrumb-like consistency.
Mix in the grated cheese.
With a cold flat bladed knife, mix the ingredients whilst pouring in half of the water and, little by little, mix the ingredients into a soft dough.
The dough should not be sticky but should leave the bowl clean around the edges when mixed.
Cover with cellophane and let stand, preferably in a fridge for an hour.
Lightly cover your work surface with flour and place the dough on the flour.
With a floured rolling pin, roll out the pastry to approximately ¼" or 6 mm thick to your desired shape / size.
Using Self Raising flour makes the flour lighter as it actually rises during baking.
For a more solid pastry, plain flour can be used.
Bake as per the recipe instructions, usually 180 / 350 / gas4 for around 30 minutes

Sweet Shortcrust Pastry

I use this recipe for most of my sweet pies, but it can go well with some savoury fillings if you use half the amount of sugar.

Ingredients.
1lb / 500g White Self Raising Flour
8 oz / 250g Cold Vegan or other Butter
2 Level Tablespoons Icing / Powdered sugar (Adjust to taste)
3 1/2 fl oz / 100ml Really Cold Water (approximately)
Pinch salt and white pepper

Method
Make sure your hands and all utensils are nice and cold before you start.
Sift the flour, salt and pepper into a mixing bowl.
Cut the butter into cubes and rub into the dry ingredients to form a breadcrumb-like consistency.
With a cold flat bladed knife, mix the powdered sugar with the other dry ingredients whilst pouring in half of the water and, little by little, mix the ingredients into a soft dough.
The dough should not be sticky but should leave the bowl clean around the edges when mixed.
Cover with cellophane and let stand, preferably in a fridge for an hour.

Lightly cover your work surface with flour and place the dough on the flour.

With a floured rolling pin, roll out the pastry to approximately ¼" or 6 mm thick to your desired shape / size.

Using Self Raising flour makes the flour lighter as it actually rises during baking.

For a more solid pastry, plain flour can be used.

Bake as per the recipe instructions, usually 180 / 350 / gas 4 for around 30 minutes

Pie Recipes

St Mary's Sausagemeat, Apple and Onion Pie.

Kindly sent in by Anne Ruddy one of the Curator / Guides at the Lhaidhay Croft Museum

Ingredients
1lb Sausage meat
2 cooking apples, peeled and sliced
2 onions, peeled and sliced
A little brown sugar
1 large egg, beaten
1 small egg, beaten
A little grated cheese.
6oz Shortcrust Pastry -
    6oz self-raising flour
    3oz butter
    1 small egg, beaten

Method
Pastry: rub the fat into the flour. Bind together with the beaten egg. Roll out to line a pie dish.

Pie filling: alternate layers of apple and onion slices in the lined dish, sprinkling a little brown sugar over the apple layers.
Mix the large beaten egg into the sausage meat. Carefully place over the layered apples and onion. Glaze with the small beaten egg and lightly sprinkle the top with a little grated cheese.
Cook on a baking tray at 370f / 165c for approximately 45 minutes. Serve piping hot with vegetables and gravy, also lovely served cold for supper or a picnic!

Shepherd's Pie

Ingredients
1lb / 500g Mince (I use vegan mince for this but you can use meat, traditionally it should be mutton or lamb)
1 Onion diced
1 Tablespoon Oil for frying
350 ml Good stock (vegetable or meat)
1 heaped teaspoon Yeast extract
1 level teaspoon dried Sage
½ level teaspoon Marjoram
¼ level teaspoon Black Pepper

For the topping -
1lb / 500g Floury (Potatoes not peeled - for the best taste)
2 oz / 50g Butter
2 Tablespoons Cream or milk
Pepper to season

Method
Fry the onions in the oil until they are brown and caramelised, put aside.
In a large saucepan, mix the mince with the herbs and add the fried onion, stir well and simmer over a low heat for five minutes, stirring constantly to prevent burning.
Add the stock and stir in well. Simmer for fifteen to twenty minutes until the mince is thoroughly cooked. Allow to stand whilst the potatoes are cooking. This allows the flavours to soak into the mince and gives a good flavour.

Cover the washed but not pealed potatoes with boiling water and continue to boil until tender.
Drain off the water (I keep this and use in gravy and soups) and place the pan of potatoes on a heatproof surface. Cut the potatoes in half.
If you have a potato ricer, put the potatoes, cut side down in the ricer and it will leave the skins behind, if not, then carefully remove the skins and put back into

the saucepan ready for mashing. Mash or rice the potatoes until smooth.

Add the butter, cream / milk and pepper and beat until smooth.

Place the mince in a greased ovenproof dish, with some of the juices but not all as these will bubble up with the heat and make the pie unattractive.

Carefully spoon the mashed potato over the mince, I usually cover the edges first then move to the centre. Score the surface with a fork to make ridges around the circumference of the potato, ending up in the middle.

Place the pie in a preheated oven, 180 / 350 / gas 4 for around 30 to 45 minutes. I like to then put the pie under the grill for 10 minutes to crisp the potato topping.

Serve piping hot with fresh vegetables and gravy or, as we used to when I was young, just with bread and butter and brown sauce.

The unused potato skins can be baked with the pie on a baking tray with a little oil and a little salt rubbed into them and served with the Shepherd's Pie, nice and crispy.

Author's Note - If using a dried vegetarian mince, such as TVP, hydrate well before adding to the pan.

Forfar Bridies

Ingredients

1lb / 500g beef. This can be replaced with vegan 'not beef' chunks
1 large Onion (optional)
Pinch of Salt & Black Pepper
1 1/2lbs Shortcrust Pastry (see pastry recipe at the beginning of this section)
1 tsp mustard powder
3 Tablespoons stock (beef or vegetable)

Method
Cut the beef into ½" / 1 cm cubes or use precut vegan options.
Put in a bowl and mix with the Chopped Onion, mustard powder, salt & Pepper and mix well. Allow to stand for a little while to allow the seasoning to soak into the filling. Add the stock and stir in well.

Divide the pastry in to six equal pieces and roll out into circles or use a plate to cut out the circles from the pastry, ideally around 8" / 20cm diameter.
Using a little water, brush around the circumference of the pastry to allow it to stick when sealing.
Spoon 1/6 of your mixture into one half only of the pastry. Press the edges together and crimp down with a

fork to ensure a seal. Brush the top of the Bridies with either egg or milk (can be non dairy milk).

Place all your Bridies on a greased baking tray or two and bake in a preheated oven, 200 / 400 / gas 6 for 35 to 40 minutes until golden brown.

Can be enjoyed hot or cold, on their own or with salad, chips, mushy peas and gravy or fresh cooked vegetables such as mashed potatoes, turnips and kale for an authentic Scottish feast. I like to eat mine on their own when they are just warm!!

Fish Recipes

Fish made up a small proportion of Crofter's diets in the early days, it was often swapped for cheese or butter and could be dried for use throughout the winter. One of the most common fish was Mackerel which was abundant in the waters on the Coast of Scotland. During the potato blight years, crofters could be seen on the beaches, collecting shellfish to help sustain themselves through bad times. Unfortunately, it often caused dysentery and bad stomachs due to not being cooked or cleaned thoroughly.

Crofter's Hot Pot

Ingredients
4 Large Herring fillets
4 medium Potatoes sliced thinly
2large Onions, sliced
2 oz Butter
Salt & Pepper

Method
Season fillets well and place half of them in a buttered dish.
Layer the fillets with Onion, then Sliced potatoes.
Season and dab with butter.
Repeat layers until all is used, finishing with the potato layer.
Dab with butter and season well.

Cover well and bake for 50 minutes to an hour 425F / 220C/ 200C fan / Gas mark 7
Remove cover and bake a further 10 – 15 minutes to allow the potatoes to brown.
Serve hot with seasonal vegetables

Crappit Heids
Recipe kindly sent in by Peter Gray

I have seen several recipes similar to this one and have to say, it must have been popular with crofters and fisher folk alike, especially with their lack of choice in ingredients. Not probably a dish that is likely to be seen in more modern times but well worthy of a space in this recipe book.

Ingredients
100g fine ground oatmeal
1/2 small brown onion, very finely chopped
25g unsalted butter
1 tbsp milk
1 tsp sea salt
black pepper
8 haddock heads
Butter for greasing

Method
In a mixing bowl rub the butter into the oatmeal and the onion. Season with salt and pepper, and bind with milk.

Take a walnut sized piece of stuffing and wedge it into the cavity underneath the eyes. Place the fish heads in the stew pan so the mouths are facing up.

Pour over enough water to just cover the base of the pot. Put the lid on and simmer gently over a medium heat for 30 minutes. Serve hot.

"The haddocks were cleaned, split open, and put into a tub with salt for a few hours. The oil being extracted from the livers in the frying pan, the browned cracklings were mixed with oatmeal, shred onions and pepper into a dough; with this the haddock-heads were stuffed, boiled for two or three hours, and then we had "crappit heads" — a dish which no epicure need despise. I don't think that in after life I ever supped so satisfactorily as I have done on the "haddock heads" of long, long ago."

Attributed to "A contributor to the Scotsman." Column entitled "Recollections of Christmas or Yule in the North of Scotland Sixty Years Ago.

Cullen Skink

This is probably one of the most popular soup recipes in the Scottish Highlands, it is very tasty and filling. I create a similar soup using smoked vegan bacon, with a little hickory smoke liquid, although not quite the same, it does impart a lovely smoky flavour and is, of course vegan.

Ingredients
1lb / 500g Smoked Haddock
1 medium onion finely chopped
8oz / 250g mashed potato
2 oz / 60g Buttermilk
350ml milk
1 Bay Leaf
Parsley (preferably fresh) Separate the stalks from the leaves.
Salt & Pepper to taste

Method

Put the milk, parsley stalks and Bay Leaf into a large saucepan.

Bring to a simmer and place the Haddock in the liquid. Bring to the boil gently and turn down to a simmer for approximately 3 – 4 minutes.

Remove the pan from the heat and set aside for 5 – 10 minutes

Remove the Haddock from the juice with a slotted spatula and set aside.

Strain the liquid to remove the Bay Leaf and Parsley stalks.

In another pan, add the butter and onion and cook gently over a low heat until the onions are translucent.

Add the Milk liquid to the pan with the potatoes, simmer and stir until the soup begins to thicken.

Flake the Haddock in to the soup in bite size pieces, discarding any bones.

Simmer gently and add the remaining chopped Parsley leaves. Do not over stir as this will break up the Haddock pieces.

After 5 minutes or so, season with salt & pepper then serve in warmed bowls with fresh crusty bread.

Smoked Haddock Kedgeree

Ingredients
2 Smoked Haddock fillets
8oz Boiled Rice
4 oz Buttermilk
2 Hard-boiled Eggs
2 oz Chopped Mushrooms
¼ tsp Cayenne Pepper
Chopped fresh Parsley to garnish
Salt & Pepper

Method
Melt the butter in a saucepan and cook the mushrooms until soft.
Add the flaked haddock, rice and Cayenne Pepper and heat through thoroughly.
Serve hot, garnished with rings of boiled Eggs and fresh Parsley.
Please Note: The rice in the recipe is already cooked once, it needs to be eaten hot and not reheated twice.

Herrings in Oatmeal

Ingredients
4 Herring approximately 8oz / 250g each with heads and bones removed.
4 – 5 oz / 125 – 150g Medium Oatmeal
4 Rashers Streaky Bacon, cut into strips
60ml / 4 Tablespoons Milk
1oz / 30G Cooking fat.
Salt and Black Pepper

Method
Pour the milk on to a dinner plate and the oatmeal on to another plate beside it.
Season the fillets well.
Dip each Herring in the milk to cover both sides. Quickly transfer to the Oatmeal and press well to allow the Oatmeal to stick. Turn it over and repeat.
Melt the cooking fat in a large skillet or frying pan and fry the bacon strips until crisp.

Remove the bacon strips from the pan and keep warm. Place the coated Herring into the hot fat and fry for approximately two minutes each side.
Place the cooked Herring on to your dinner plate and sprinkle with the bacon strips, serve with boiled potatoes, fresh veg or Skirlie.

Soused Herring

Ingredients
12 Herring Fillets (Boned and scaled)
2 Small Onions, cut into rings
½ pint mixed water and vinegar
1 Tablespoon Pickling Spice
4 Bay Leaves
Salt & Pepper

Method
Season fillets well and roll quite tightly, then place in an oven proof dish. Stacking them closely together.
Pour over the water / vinegar liquid and sprinkle with pickling spice.
Garnish with the onion rings and bay leaves.
Cover well (if you don't have a lid, use baking foil)
Bake in the oven for 45 minutes 180 / 350 / gas 4.
Serve with Wholemeal / Beremeal Bannocks or New Potatoes.

Partan Bree

Ingredients
1 large boiled crab
3 oz / 85g Long grain rice
1 pint stock
1 pint milk
¼ pint single cream
Dash of Anchovy Essence
Salt & Pepper

Method
Pick all the meat from the cooked crab, separating the white from the brown.
Boil the milk and stock in a pan, mix in the brown meat and simmer for ten minutes.
Mash or liquidise the mixture.
Return to the heat and add the Anchovy Essence and season with salt & pepper.
Add the white crab meat and the cream and stir in gently.
Serve hot with crust bread or bannocks.

Haggamuggie

A sort of piscatorial haggis.

Ingredients

A whole large fish.
Toasted fine Oatmeal
Salt & Pepper to taste

Method

Wash the muggie (stomach) of a fish, tie the small end tightly with fine string, fill two-thirds full with a stuffing made by breaking up the liver with the fingers, mixing it with an equal quantity of lightly toasted, fine oatmeal, and seasoning with salt and pepper. Tie the open end about an inch down so that it does not slip off. Plunge into boiling salted water and boil for twenty-five or thirty minutes. Drain and serve with hot potatoes. The Muggie is eaten along with its contents.

Meat Recipes

Very little meat would be eaten by the Crofter's family as most would be traded and sold. Here are a few recipes using scraps and left overs which made a hearty meal.

Haggis

What recipe book would be complete without a recipe for Haggis, probably the most commonly known Scottish dish. Although there are many versions of this traditional dish as it was generally made from the less quality meat products, the basis would be the same.

Basic traditional Haggis

Ingredients.
Pluck of sheep (Heart, liver, lungs / lites)
Stomach of sheep (Paunch)
1/2lb suet
2 Onions
Oatmeal
Salt & Pepper to taste

Method
1. Wash intestines in cold water, bring to boil, scrape and clean.
Leave overnight in clean water.
2. Wash stomach and put in pan of boiling water. Boil

for two hours with windpipe draining into a jar.
3. Cut off windpipe, mince best part of lungs and heart, remove gristle and grate best parts of liver.
4. Add toasted oatmeal, minced suet and onions, 2 teaspoons of salt, 1 teaspoon of pepper, herbs and enough of the liquid into which stomach has been boiled to moisten.
5. Almost fill the stomach bag, keeping fat or smooth side inside. Sew then prick well.
6. Place on plate in pot of boiling water. Boil gently for three hours.
Serve the Haggis turned out of the paunch on to a large dish and serve with mashed swede.

Inky Pinky

I was told about this recipe by a good friend who was born in Glasgow, Iris could remember the name 'Inky Pinky' as a child because it also meant 'wayward' or 'naughty' child. Times were hard for her family and quite often the meat was almost like rubber as it was not the best cut available but a mere scrap from the butcher's shop. Iris has told me of many times when she, as a child, had to scavenge for food for the table, I'm sure her experiences were similar to those of the crofters in bad times. When there was nothing else to eat, then chips were her go to meal!

Ingredients
Left over Lamb or Beef (any meat in reality)
2 Carrots Boiled and sliced
2 Small Onions, chopped
1lb Mashed potatoes

Method
Place the sliced Carrots in an oven proof dish or saucepan.
Add the chopped Onions and then a layer of sliced meat.
Combine with a covering of good gravy and add a little flour to thicken.
Heat thoroughly and serve with hot mashed potato.

Stovies

Ingredients
Leftover meat- beef or lamb – Meat to be cubed
2lb / 900g Potatoes
1 Large onion
1-2tbsp Beef dripping / Butter / lard
200ml Beef stock
Dash of milk or butter
Salt and pepper to taste
Leftover vegetables (carrots, swede)

Method

Chop your onion, cube your meat, wash and peel your potatoes before cutting into thick slices and set aside. Heat 1-2tbsp beef dripping over a medium heat in your pan. Ideally you would use beef dripping from the previous night leftovers but I know it's not always possible so you can buy a block of beef dripping at the supermarket, alternatively, use some butter or lard if you prefer.

Once the beef dripping has melted, add your chopped onion to the pan and sauté for around 3-5 minutes in the fat until softened and translucent. Don't worry about any browning, this adds to the flavour.

Next, layer your raw potatoes in the pan and give a quick stir to coat in the onions and fat.

Add 200ml beef stock to the pan. If needed, add some cold water until the liquid is covering around 2/3 of the potatoes.

Place the lid on the pan and cook this on a medium heat for around 5-10 minutes.

Ideally, use the previous night's roast, add those and all the leftover scrapings and flavourings now. If you are using fresh meat, then add that on top of the potatoes now.

Do not stir with the potatoes!

If you are adding fresh veg, do so now but again, do not stir.

Season with some salt and pepper before bringing the liquid to a boil. Once boil has been reached, set heat to a gentle simmer, cover the pan with your lid, leaving to cook for approximately 30-45 minutes.

If you are adding precooked veg, do so around 10 minutes before readiness.

The potatoes will begin to fall apart and the liquid and juices in the pan will have reduced. You don't want the potatoes to be mushy, just soft enough to fall into a mash.

The consistency should be of lumpy and soft potato pieces.

Remove pan from the heat and add a little milk or butter before giving a quick stir through. Give it a taste and add some more salt and pepper if needed.

Allow to stand for around 30 minutes to allow the flavours to settle.

After this, place them back on the hob on a high heat, stirring again before serving piping hot!

Marag dubh (Black Pudding)

The Isle of Lewis crofters knew black pudding by its Scottish Gaelic name, "marag dubh", with "dubh" meaning "black".
Many crofting *wifeys disliked the cleaning out of pans after making this important dish. I can imagine it to be unpleasant, especially without the help of modern wash liquids!
*('Wifey' is a Highland term for any woman)

Ingredients
1lb suet (finely chopped)
1lb oatmeal
2 onions
Fresh blood (may be watered down)
Salt and pepper

Method
1. Place all dry ingredients in a bowl. Mix and blend with fresh sheep's blood.
2. Stuff mixture into casing and tie well.
3. Place in large pan, cover with boiling water, and boil gently for three hours.
4. Remove black puddings and allow to cool.
5. Cut into slices as required and fry in hot fat.

Cheese, Cream & Milk Recipes

Milk formed an important part of the Crofter's diet, with most crofters having at least one cow. Much of the produce would be sold or swapped for other needed items, such as fish or occasionally meat. Soft cheese, such as Crowdie, a soft cheese not unlike our modern cream cheeses, would be very popular as it was quick and easy to make with the use of rennet.

Crowdie

Ingredients
1/5 ltrs Milk (Whole milk not skimmed)
Juice of 1 Lemon – Traditionally Rennet was used
Double Cream
Salt & Pepper
Oatmeal to garnish

Method
Add the milk to a heavy bottomed saucepan and warm gently
Add the Lemon juice and continue to warm the milk but do not boil
You will see the milk begin to separate into curds and whey.
Leave on the heat until the liquid has completely separated.
Remove from the heat.
Ladle the curds (more solid of the two) into a clean muslin cloth or bag. If using a cloth, bring the corners

together and tie with a string before hanging over the bowl.
Hang the bag over a bowl and allow to drain for 3-4 hours.
Remove the curd ball from the bag and place in a bowl.
Add a small amount of the cream and mix well, it should be the consistency of a soft cream cheese.
Add the salt & pepper, form into a 'pat' or round and sprinkle with the oatmeal to create a thin layer either on top of the cheese or roll the curds in the oatmeal if you have a thicker consistency. You can add herbs such as parsley, marjoram, thyme finely chopped onion or garlic to taste for an alternative flavour.
Serve with oatcakes.

Fuarag
This recipe was kindly provided by George and Nan Bethune

Ingredients
1 Tablespoon oatmeal
One cupful of fresh cream

Method
1. Add the oatmeal to the cream and stir well.
2. Sugar may also be added to taste.
2. Eat at once. This makes an appetising breakfast but there are some who would take it at any time of day.

Side Dishes & Other Savouries

Skirlie

The ingredients for this dish are quite basic but they make a really tasty and filling side dish or just with mashed potatoes or even with a breakfast. It can also be used as a stuffing.

Ingredients
2 Onions roughly chopped
3oz / 85g Butter / Margarine
5oz / 150g Oatmeal
2 tsp chopped fresh thyme
Salt & Pepper to taste

Method
Melt the fat in a skillet or frying pan.
Add the Onion, stir and cook on a low heat until well browned, ideally it should be covered to hold in all the flavours.
Add enough Oatmeal to make a fairly thick consistency.
Add the Thyme, Salt and Pepper.
Continue to cook on a low heat to prevent burning for around 5 – 8 minutes.

Serve hot as an accompaniment to many savoury dishes.

Clapshot

Ingredients
1lb / 500g Floury Potatoes, peeled and diced for boiling
1lb / 500g Turnip (or swede) peeled and diced for boiling
2 ½ oz / 75g Butter or 75ml Single Cream
2 Tablespoons Chopped fresh Chives (or spring onion)
Salt & Pepper to taste.

Method
Boil the potatoes and turnips in separate pans until tender.
Drain well and turn both vegetables into one pan.
Remove from the heat and mash thoroughly until smooth.
Place back over a low heat and add the butter or cream and beat until smooth and fluffy.
Stir in the chives and seasoning.
Sprinkle a few chives on top of the mixture.
Serve immediately whilst piping hot.

As a variation, I sometimes melt grated cheese on top.

Sweet Treats

What Scottish recipe book would be complete without a section for the sweet tooth? Here we cover some of the more traditional recipes such as Tablet, Clootie Dumpling, Shortbread, Gingerbread and Cranachan plus lots more from various localities in Scotland kindly sent in by cooks of all ages.

Clootie Dumpling

Ingredients
9 oz / 250g Mixed dried Fruit
6oz / 170g Shredded Suet
6 fl oz / 170ml Milk
5oz / 150g / Self Raising Flour
5 oz / 150g Fresh Breadcrumbs
5oz / 150g Soft Dark Brown Sugar
2 Eggs or egg substitute
2 Tablespoons / 30ml Marmalade
Grated zest of 1 Orange & 1 Lemon
1 Tablespoon / 15ml Black Treacle or Molasses
1 Teaspoon Ground Ginger
1 Teaspoon Ground Cinnamon

Method
In a large mixing bowl, mix all the ingredients together thoroughly.
Using a large tea towel or piece of muslin which has been dipped in boiling water, place it over a large

pudding bowl and sift a small amount of flour over the fabric.

Transfer the 'dumpling mix' into the cloth and bring the corners and sides together, squeezing the dough into a round shape but allowing some space to allow the dumpling to expand. Tie the top securely with string.

In a large saucepan or pressure cooker, place a metal trivet or up turned sandwich tin on the bottom. Place the pudding in its cloth on the trivet and cover the dumpling with boiling water.

Boil for around 3 hours until firm, checking the water level regularly and topping up if needed.

Remove carefully from the boiling water and place on a plate or serving dish.

Cut the string and remove the fabric, dust with sugar and serve hot with custard.

I have also used Clootie Dumpling the next day, sliced and fried with a Scottish Breakfast, it was lovely!

Broonie / Gingerbread

Ingredients
6oz / 170g Plain Flour
6oz / 170g Medium Oatmeal
10 fl oz / 280ml Buttermilk/ yoghurt
3oz /85g Dark Brown Sugar

3oz / 85g Butter
3oz / 85g Raisins (optional)
2 Tablespoons / 30ml Black Treacle
1 Egg (or vegan substitute)
2 Teaspoons / 10ml Ground Ginger
½ Teaspoon / 2.5g Bicarbonate of soda
½ Teaspoon / 2.5g White Pepper

Method
Preheat oven to 180 / 350 / gas 4 Grease a 4" x 8" load tin and line with greaseproof paper.

Sift the flour, oatmeal, bicarbonate of soda, ginger and pepper into a mixing bowl.
Gently melt the butter, sugar and black treacle together in a saucepan then stir in the yoghurt / buttermilk until it has combined. If using raisins, stir in and let them soak for a little while. Beat in the egg or egg substitute when the liquid is just warm so as not to curdle.
Pour the warm liquid into the dry ingredients and stir well to combine and make a soft but fairly thick batter. Pour into the lined loaf tin and bake for around an hour. (If the top of the loaf begins to burn, lay some greaseproof paper over it and turn the oven down a little.
When the loaf is firm to the touch in the centre, remove from the oven.
Allow to cool for 20 minutes or so then lift out of the tin and remove the greaseproof paper. Place on a wire

rack. Once cold, place in a tin and keep for 3 – 5 days, this will make the top of the loaf turn wonderfully sticky!
Orange peel, cinnamon or crystallised ginger pieces can also be added.

Beremeal Gingerbread

Ingredients
6oz / 170g Plain Flour
6oz/ 170g Beremeal
4oz /115g Brown Sugar
3 oz/ 85g Butter
2oz / 60g Raisins
2oz / 60g Black Treacle
2oz / 60g Golden Syrup
5fl oz / 150ml Milk (Plant milk is fine)
1 Egg (Egg substitute works well, such as 4 Tablespoons Apple Sauce or the same quantity of mashed ripe banana)
1 Heaped teaspoon ground ginger
1 level Tsp Bicarbonate of Soda
¼ tsp white pepper

Method
Heat your oven to 160 / 325 / gas 3
Grease and line two 1lb loaf tins
Sift the flour, ginger and bicarbonate of soda into a large mixing bowl, stir together.
Add the beremeal and combine well.
In a saucepan, gently heat the butter, treacle and syrup until the butter melts and the liquid is warm but not hot.
Add ¾ of the milk and stir well.
Make a well in the centre of your dry ingredients and gently stir in the warm liquid until it is well mixed.
Add your egg or egg substitute and the raisins.
Divide the mixture evenly between the two loaf tins.
Do not bang the tins as this will flatten the cake
Place in the centre of the oven and bake for 30 minutes until firm on top.
To check it is completely cooked, insert a skewer half way through the centre, if it comes out clean, it is cooked.
Cool for half an hour in the tins then, after removing any of the greaseproof paper and cool on a rack.
This cake is best left in sealed container for 4-5 days to allow the treacle and syrup to do its work to form a gloriously sticky top.
This cake freezes well and any dried crumbs can be used in Ice Cream or sprinkled on top of overnight oats.

Beremeal Shortbread

Ingredients
12oz / 340g Self Raising flour
4oz / 115g Beremeal
8oz / 225g Butter
8oz / 225g Caster Sugar
1/2tsp Salt

Method
Mix all the dry ingredients (except the sugar) together in a large bowl.
Rub in the butter until it looks like fine bread crumbs, stir in the sugar.
Mix the ingredients together to form a ball of dough. Turn out on to a floured surface and knead until the dough is smooth and not sticky. Seal in cling wrap and chill in the refrigerator for around 1 - 2 hours.
Roll out to approximately ¼" thick
Cut into rounds approximately 3" diameter and place on a baking tray.
Place in a preheated oven 180 / 160 (fan) bake for 12 – 15 minutes until golden brown. When removing from the oven sift a little extra caster sugar on top of the biscuits. Leave to harden on the baking tray then fully cool on a wire rack.

Traditional Scottish Shortbread

Ingredients
12 oz / 340g Plain Flour
8oz / 250g Cold Butter
4oz / 125g Caster Sugar
Pinch Salt

Method
Preheat your oven to 160c / 325f / gas mark 3
Lightly grease a baking tray or two sandwich tins

Sift the flour and salt into a large bowl and rub in the butter.
Mix in the sugar (apart from 2 teaspoons).
Knead into a soft dough, cut in two pieces and turn one piece out on to a lightly floured piece of greaseproof paper which should be slightly larger than your baking tray or sandwich tin.
Roll out each piece to approximately 1/2" thick.
Repeat with the second half of the dough.
Carefully transfer on to a lightly greased baking tray. You can use a sandwich tin and simply press out the ball of dough to form a flat circle if you prefer. Prick all over with a fork and score into 6 – 8 petticoat tails from the centre (depends on how generous your portions need to be!)
Place in the centre of the oven for approximately 30 – 40 minutes or until a light golden brown.

When you remove from the oven, sift the caster sugar over the shortbread.

Allow to cool on the baking tray or in the sandwich tins so that they do not break when moving. Place on a wire rack to store in an airtight tin for completely cool.

Escape Cake
Kindly sent in by Anne Ruddy

Ingredients
8oz butter
8oz soft brown sugar
14oz mixed fruit
2 large eggs
1/2 pint cider
1lb self-raising flour

Method
Gently simmer butter, the fruit, cider, and the sugar in a pan. Allow to cool.
Whisk eggs together.
When fruit mixture has cooled, stir in the whisked eggs and the flour.
Bake in a fully lined cake tin at 160 F / 140c for approximately 1.5 hours, or until a knitting needle pushed into the centre of the cake comes out clean.
Would make an excellent Christmas cake, with marzipan!

Cranachan

Ingredients
1.5 oz / 40g oatmeal (pin head is ideal)
8 fl oz / 250ml Whipping cream / Double Cream
2 tbsp clear honey, plus extra to serve
1-2 tbsp whisky, to taste
4.5 oz / 125g raspberries, plus extra to serve

Method
Put the oatmeal in a clean skillet or frying pan. Gently toast for around 20 minutes, turning regularly.
Whip the Double Cream until is thick but not quite forming stiff peaks.
Add the Whisky and Honey to taste.
Saving a few Raspberries, fold in the raspberries carefully.

Before serving, sprinkle some of the toasted Oatmeal on top and add one or two large Raspberries to finish

I don't think we could possibly go any further without a few recipes for the sweetest of confections made in Scotland, Scottish Tablet. It was probably not the most common food item for the Crofters but I imagine for a very special treat, it would be treasured! It is similar to fudge but has a more crumbly, very creamy texture that melts in the mouth, not for the feint hearted or for those looking for a healthy treat but a must for anyone who loves very sweet - sweets.

Scottish Tablet

Ingredients
1lb 2oz / 500g Granulated Sugar
6 fl oz / 170ml Water
60g Butter (vegan butter is fine)
3 Tablespoons / 45ml Sweetened Condensed Milk (coconut sweetened condensed milk is a great substitute)

Method
You will need a large heavy bottomed pan for this recipe. I use my old pressure cooker.
Place all the ingredients in the pan.
Stir over a gently heat until the sugar has dissolved and does not make a gritty sound when stirred.
Bring to the boil and simmer until it reaches soft ball stage 116 / 240 degrees. If you don't have a confectioner's thermometer, this is when a small amount dropped into very cold water turns into a soft caramel texture that can be rolled in to a soft ball.
Remove from the heat once it has reached the soft ball stage and put on a heat proof surface.
Beat with a wooden spoon (or a mixer for ease) for around 5 minutes, the mixture will become opaque

rather than shin. Pour into a buttered tin 7 x 11 inches / 18 x 28 cm. Mark into squares before it sets and eat once cold.

This can be stored in air tight containers for around a week (if it lasts that long!)

Butterscotch

Ingredients
8 oz / 250g Demerara Sugar
2oz / 60g Butter
1 Cup Water
1 Tablespoon Vinegar

Method
Place all the ingredients in a heavy bottomed pan and heat gently until the sugar has dissolved.
Boil briskly for around 5 minutes without stirring until the mixture thickens. It should reach the hard crack temperature of around 148 / 300 degrees.
You can test the mixture to see if it forms a hard cracking texture when dropped into very cold water.
Pour into a buttered tin. You can score into squares or oblongs just before it sets or if you forget, just hit the underneath of the tin with a rolling pin and it will crack the Butterscotch for a more rustic finish.

Beers, Wines and Other Drink

Fisherman's Punch
Kindly sent in by - Minmum and Doosedrop

Ingredients
One half bottle red wine - cheap!
One large un-waxed orange
Soft brown sugar
Cinnamon
Cloves

Method
Prick the orange all over with a fork.
Stick six cloves into the orange.
Pour half a bottle of red wine into a saucepan, add 1 tablespoon of soft brown sugar and 1 teaspoon of cinnamon.
Simmer gently for fifteen minutes.
Serve and enjoy!

Deoch bhan (Oatmeal drink)

Ingredients
2 Pints Hot Water
2 Tbsp Cold Water
2 tablespoons oatmeal
Pinch of salt
Half ounce butter

Method
1. Mix the oatmeal and salt with cold water.
2. Add butter.
3. Pour 2 pints of hot water over it.
4. Leave it beside the fire covered with a plate or saucer to keep it hot.

Must always be drunk hot!

Athol Brose

Ingredients
One bottle of Scotch whisky
1/2 Pint of double cream / Plant based double cream works well too.
450g of clear Scottish honey or vegan Honey
One handful of fine ground oatmeal

Method.
Combine the oatmeal and whisky in a shallow container. Cover with linen and leave in a cool place for several hours or overnight.
Remove the liquids from your oatmeal and whisky mixture. Use linen or a spoon and strainer to squeeze every last drop of whisky out of the oatmeal solids. Discard the oats.
This step is optional, some more traditional recipes don't use cream, while others even recommend mixing

the cream with egg whites. This step can be used or left out as per your preference.
Add cream and stir
Gently whisk in honey, until dissolved.
Stir the final mixture well (according to tradition, this should be done with a silver spoon). Pour the brose into a bottle for storage.

Pick whichever whisky takes your fancy but a decent blend will work just as well as a good malt. I recommend that you perhaps don't use a peaty whisky as this can detract from the sweet flavour.

Athol Brose also works well as a dessert just add raspberries and drizzle over a nice ice cream.

A few words from Socially Growing Thurso Caithness

Advertisement

We are thrilled to introduce "A Taste of Crofting" by Barbara Jane Gray, a cookbook that encapsulates the essence of Scottish heritage through a delightful array of recipes. From oatmeal-based classics to sourdough wonders, this book is a treasure trove of time-honoured culinary wisdom.

At Socially Growing, our shelves proudly display the very ingredients highlighted in this cookbook. Our commitment to zero waste is reflected in our extensive collection of oats, various flours, fragrant herbs, and dried fruits, all carefully sourced from local and sustainable suppliers. By utilizing these ingredients, you not only honour the heritage of crofting but also contribute to a healthier, more eco-conscious lifestyle.

"A Taste of Crofting" isn't just about recipes; it's a journey that intertwines the rich flavours of the past with a vision for a sustainable future. Barbara Jane Gray's emphasis on locally sourced, organic produce echoes our belief in fostering a circular economy and reducing environmental impact. With each turn of the page, you'll discover not just culinary inspiration but also a deeper connection to the roots of Scottish culture and the beauty of sustainable living.

Let "A Taste of Crofting" and Socially Growing guide you on a culinary adventure that embraces the spirit of tradition and sustainability. Together, let's savour the flavours of the past and nurture a greener, more mindful tomorrow.

Socially Growing

Visit our shop and greenhouses to learn more about our social enterprise and the volunteering opportunities we have available. We are always adding new products and cater to different dietary needs.
Every purchase made with us supports Thurso Community Development Trust.

Beremeal and Barony Mill
Advertisement

Barony Mill in Birsay is totally unique, the only working water mill in Orkney and certainly the only water mill in the UK to grind bere. It has been in almost continuous use since 1873.

At Barony Mill, the power from the waterwheel drives all the machinery including the three sets of grinding stones making it very environmentally friendly.

Beremeal is milled from October to April when there is plenty of water in the nearby loch. Between May and September, we run guided tours for visitors.

Beremeal is a flour made by grinding the grain of bere, an ancient type of barley. Bere grain has been found in Neolithic tombs in Orkney, suggesting that it was grown here 4,000 years ago. Beremeal is higher in protein and lower in starch than modern barley, and also low in gluten. Beremeal is used by local bakers adding traditional flavour to bannocks, cakes and biscuits, and also exported to mainland Scotland and internationally.

Our beremeal, bere flake and bere berries, alongside a range of oatmeals, can be bought from our web shop at baronymill.com or through our stockists who are listed on the website.

Bere has also historically been used in brewing and distilling and continues to this day to produce beer and whisky with a distinctive flavour.

Stoneground
ORKNEY BEREMEAL
BARONY MILL BIRSAY
Milling for over 300 years

Bere is an ancient form of barley with a unique appearance and taste, grown and milled in Orkney throughout the centuries

100% Natural, it is wonderful for baking bannocks, scones and biscuits.

NOTHING TAKEN OUT, NOTHING ADDED IN!

www.baronymill.com

Working water mill, operated by
Birsay Heritage Trust
SCO27642